Double Your Profits

Double Your Profits

Jasmin Hajro

Jasmin Hajro

ISBN-13: 978-1723142024

ISBN-10: 1723142026

Cover design by

Jasmin Hajro

First english edition 2018

In this short but powerfull book you'll discover :

The bio of entrepreneur & author Jasmin Hajro

&

How approach your prospects in a unique and credible way
&

How to get people to visit your business & website

&

How to easily be attractively different

&

The Ultimate Winning Strategy
for entrepreneurs

With all of this, you'll double your profits.

My results in august 2017 : 32,5 sales
in september 2017 : 43,5 sales
in october 2017 : 18 sales
in november 2017 : 86 sales

If I can double my profits, so can You.

&

Plus a Bonus

The bio of author Jasmin Hajro, nice to meet you

Hello dear reader, how are you ?

Thank you for buying one of my books.

My name is Jasmin Hajro,
I was born on July 6, 1985 in Bosnia.
As refugees, we came to the Netherlands 21 years ago.
After having completed school & worked at several jobs ...

On 17 December 2012, I founded my first company:
investment firm Jasko. After a successful first year,
I unfortunately had to close that company.

After a short period of rest, unemployment and temporary work.
I started again as an entrepreneur.

On September 1, 2015, I founded establishment Hajro.

(We say establishment instead of company,
because we do a bit more then just sell stuff.
Like providing jobs,
donating to 40 different charities,
and helping people to live richer.)

Since the beginning the core activity is,
selling sets of greeting cards,
door to door.
Nowadays the product range has been expanded.

With, among other things, the selling of my 12 books.

The royalties of my books are donated to the charity:
foundation Giveth Life.
From there more than 40 other charities
receive donations.
And by buying this book, so do you.
Thank you.

My company is now part of Hajro Group,
which consists of 19 different subsidiaries,
that are part of 1 umbrella organization.
Called Energy Now (Energie Nu)

For more information about my company
& the foundation, go to www.hajrobv.nl

How to approach your prospects in a unique & credible way

Do you have a flyer, a salesletter
some offers on your website &
some Blogarticles ??

Great.

Bundle everything....
Find a printing company.
With all your writings combined,
have them print your very own Newspaper.
Include in it a few articles about some good things,
that are happening in your community.
To make it a good news newspaper.

In your own newspaper you have plenty of space to
introduce yourself.
And to present your company in the best way possible.
You also have space for fullpage ads for all your offers.

You can even sell advertising space to other companies

(That printing company will print about 5000 copies
of Your newspaper for about 200 dollar)
Negotiate a sweet deal.

Now find someone to deliver Your newspaper to your prospects.

(Pay 5 cents or something for every delivered copy
of Your newspaper)

How to get people to visit your business & website

Are you doing any marketing & advertising ?

Knock it off.
Stop doing it.
Stop everything.

Now you have saved yourself some money.

Then order about 13 books on copywriting.
Study them, 1 book a month or 1 book a week.

After you've read them all 13...

Now write a 1 or 2 pagesalesletter
Introduce yourself,
introduce your company,
tell what you can do for the prospect :
Your offer & the benefits they will enjoy from having or using it.

Then give them a reason to visit your website;
for example because your giving away a free report or
free Ebook

Give them a reason to visit your store by adding

a discount coupon,
which they can only use for a limited time.

Because no one can tell about your company
and offer,
as enthusiastically as you...

You have to write your persuasive sales letter.

Then have it printed & delivered to your prospects.

If you want people to look at it,
put your letters in envelopes.

If you want to get their attention,
repeat the process several times.

How to easily be attractively different

Write your book or booklet.

And position yourself as an expert.
If you know more about a subject than I do,
then you are an expert to me,
regarding that subject.

So write about what you are good at,
or what you know a lot about.

Describe your experiences as a salesperson,
or as an entrepreneur.

Describe your life lessons.

Then you publish your book,
via barnes&noble press & lulu.com &
createspace.com & kobo.com

Your book will then be available for sale in various
bookstores in several countries.
Including Amazon.com & barnes&noble

Your book becomes a marketing tool for you,
and for your company.

Mention in it or on your book, your web address or
that of your company.

Make yourself a familiar person.
People prefer to buy from a celebrity /
well-known person.

That's why you see celebrities and wellknown people
in advertisements,

praising products.

If you want to very easily create & publish your first book....

Then put all the texts on your website,
in a pdf.
Write and add some things, like your flyer and blogarticles.
And your first book is ready
to be published.
The advantage of this is that you have copyright
on the texts on your website and your other writings.
And,
you have went through the process of creating &
publishing a book already once.

So you can now more easily create your 2nd book .

Write down how your last year went.

And publish that as your second book.

Do the same for 8 other years of your life.

Write down how that year of your life went for you and publish it

as a book or booklet.

Keep a journal, so you can easily make a book out of this year

This is my businesscard :

Go to www.hajrobv.nl

and check out the background of my website.

Then go to my books

and check out the covers.

Now give your businesscards,

your website &

your books the same corporate identity .

SelfPublish your books with amazon's

kindle direct publishing & create space

+

with barnes and noble press

+

kobo.com

You now have a recognzable brand, that stands out.

(In your books you can ask the readers to visit your website for

a promotional freebie)

With your company you can start to support 20 local charities,

to differentiate your business even more..

Don't get overwhelmed

Put all the mail you get in a drawer.

Once a month, open and read your mail.

Only once a month.

And your email,
leave it.

And open your emailbox once a week and read it.

Don't worry nobody is gonna die,
while you create peace in your mind
& life.

Thus creating more free time,
to do the important things.
Like earning money.

" By the way, I started my first company in 2012.

I have made more than 700 sales since

1 September 2015 so far.

So I have a track record
in sales and business,
and I know what I'm talking about. "

" As you have probably already understood,
I earn my money by selling for my own company.
That's my work. "

The proceeds from my books go to charity.

I write from experience,
I write to help people move forward
in their lives and business "

The Ultimate Winning Strategy for entrepreneurs

How do we measure success in business?
With monetary points, with earned euro's or dollars.

What is a successful business?

Successful entrepreneurship =
selling a lot

We are therefore successfully running our business,
if we sell a lot.

So success in doing business = selling a lot
(many sales realized / many sales closed)

Because sales means profits.

So what is the Ultimate Winning Strategy in business?

First we start with the concept,
then you get 2 examples from real life

Have you noticed that supermarkets are open 7 days a week?

Supermarkets may be a less good example,
because we just have to eat and drink.

Have you been to the Esso gas station?
(Part of Exxon mobil corporation)
The Esso gas station has a shop with staff,
and is open 24 hours a day, 7 days a week.

And no, even if it seems that we need petrol,
the Esso could also have become a self-service gas station,
where you fill your tank and pay with a creditcard.

But the Esso has a shop with staff, 24/7 .

What do the supermarkets do every day?

<u>They make sales and profits.</u>
<u>Every day !</u>

What does the Esso do every day and night?

The Esso makes sales day and night,
every day.
<u>So the Esso makes profits,</u>
<u> every day and night of the year</u>

The supermarkets and the Esso are successful
because they realize sales every day
and thus make profits every day.

<u>The Ultimate Winning Strategy for entrepreneurs</u>
<u>is</u>
<u> making profits every day.</u>

Make a profit every day of the year.

You do that by selling every day,
and by daily closing sales.

Your advantage over your competition

If you sell every day & make profits every day,
do you than have an advantage over companies
who only make profits 5 days a week?

<u>Example 1 from real life</u>

I have been selling from Monday, September 18, 2017
untill Wednesday, September 27, 2017,
10 days in a row,
and made 22 sales in total.

So every day I made sales & I made profits everyday.

That is the Ultimate Winning Strategy for entrepreneurs in action.
(in the real life of running your business)

Well if we are honest,
then we know that the transaction value
of sets of greeting cards is modest.
And therefore the profit per sale is also.

But do not be turned off by those numbers ...
You will soon receive a real life example from someone who
made 1 million.

<u>This was to make you understand the successful Concept
of the Ultimate Winning Strategy for entrepreneurs
and that you see proven that it works.</u>

You now understand that Concept,
you have seen some examples of companies
applying the Ultimate Winning Strategy.
You have seen a real life example
from me I have proven to you that it works.

And you are 100% assured that the Ultimate Winning Strategy
works.

People do not need greeting cards
like they need food and drinks,
but they bought every day
and I made profits every day.

So it does not matter what kind of product or service you sell.

<u>The Ultimate Winning Strategy also works for you.</u>

<u>Next step</u>

You understand the Ultimate Winning Strategy for entrepreneurs,
and you know it works.

So now you are going to do it.

You are going to implement it.

I'm not asking you to work 7 days a week,
although you should do it once.
(That will boost your confidence)

You can sell from Monday to Friday &
hire someone who sells for you
from Saturday to Monday (a part-timer)

Then you will already have
sales every day and profits every day.

If I can do it alone,
then you can certainly do it with 2 people!

Are there any other ways how you can
make sales everyday & profits ever day?

Consider, think and find 20 ways,
with which you can make sales everyday

and therefore make profits everyday.

Write them down.

1 Hire a salesperson
2 Create a team of salespeople
3
4
5
6
7
8
9
10
11
12
13
14
15
16
17
18
19
20

Example 2 from real life

Go to www.youtube.nl
and watch the video of Walter Bergeron,
GKIC marketer of the year.

The video lasts about half an hour.

Pay close attention when he says: that means also on saturdays
and sundays.

(that he was selling 7 days a week and
making profits every day)

Have you seen
what the Ultimate Winning Strategy for entrepreneurs
can do for you?

Go to work,
go out selling every day & making profits every day.

Apply your 20 ways,
give your sales a boost,
make lots of profits.
Every day of the year.

I wish you a lot of succes.

Met vriendelijke groeten,

Jasmin Hajro

Hajro
Ottawastraat 19
7007 BC
Doetinchem,
the Netherlands
KvK : 65686306

www.hajrobv.nl

Selling is the lifebreath of your business.

If you set everything aside,
and just Focus on this 1 thing everyday.
Focus on making sales everyday,
you will soon double your profits.

If I can, so can You

Say : I CAN

and get to work.

P.S. If you have liked this book and got good value from it,
than would you be so kind
to recommend it to people that you know.
So that it also helps them forward.
Thank you.

<u>I would like to give you another book</u>
<u>as a gift</u>

It's called Recipe for Happiness,
and it can help you achieve your
sales and businessgoals.

Beacuse If you are more relaxed and happy,
you will be more productive

You can read it on the following pages.

Enjoy.

The Recipe for Happiness

A book has been written about a true story ...
About a man who was imprisoned in a
concentration camp at the time of Hitler,
and happy.

So, Happiness has nothing to do with your circumstances.
It has everything to do with,
your choice to be happy,
regardless of circumstances.

Choose to be happy.

Of course there are touhger times in life,
like when someone you love, dies.
That's part of life.
Those times of grief you just have to go through and process.

Processing is best done by talking about it,
to get it off your chest regularly.

Or by writing about it,
if you write down a situation or your feelings about it,
then it's on paper,
and it is less in your head.

Writing is a good outlet.

Processing is also done well by: staying busy.
Whether that is in your work or your hobby.
They say: a rolling stone does not collect moss.
So stay busy ....

Okay, now you have learned a good lesson about how to better process negative life experiences.

But you're here for the Recipe for Happiness, right?

Well, the lesson you've learned will help
to make the recipe work better for you.

Here it comes then …

You have probably read a local newspaper,
and you regularly check the news.
(the daily news on television)

Have you noticed that about 99% of it is bad news?
Only misery ..
If you did not know better,
you would think that the whole world is going to perish.

If it's a habit for you,
to watch the news every day for half an hour …

Have you ever wondered if it's healthy for you?
Does it make you happy ?
Of course not !

The easiest way to change a habit is by replacing it
with a new habit.

So from today on, instead of watching the worldly news half an
hour a day ....

Watch COMEDY for half an hour a day.

Mandatory.

Every day.

Well, now at half past eight in the evening it's not news time,
but Comedy time.

If you watch comedy, you relax & you laugh.
Sounds healthier, doesn't it?

Well, laughing every day is easy to do, right?

And replacing your old bad habit in this way,
with a nice, healthy new habit,
is probably easier than you thought.

Except for the fact that relaxation is good for you,
when you laugh, also your body makes endorphins.
Those are natural happiness substances.

Well, after 21 days of daily watching comedy,
you will have formed a new habit.

So watch Comedy every day.

You can watch a lot of standup comedy on Youtube for free.
Simple?
Sure,
but you have to do it,
every day,
until you don't have to think about it anymore,
and you start doing it automatically.

Some Happiness Ingredients in a row:

–   Watch comedy every day, at least one hour.

–   Eat ice cream, treat someone with an ice cream.

–   Work out, throw out your frustration by playing tennis or
go for a run.

–   Pee in the yard (and if you get a fine for urinating, laugh
your ass off)

–   Do not worry, life is too short for that (by staying busy,
you do not have time to worry)

–   Hug the people that you love

–   Go enjoy a cup of coffee or tea

–   Buy or save a cat or some other pet

–   When you receive money, immediately save a part of it

–   Don't let the media scare you, the world is not getting
worse, the world is getting better.

–   Sex, need I say more
(when you have sex your body also
–   produces endorphins =
those natural happiness substances)

Maybe the Recipe for Happiness
is different than you had expected....
But that doesn't matter,
the point is that it works &
that it will help you to live happier.

Do it,
it is easier
then looking with a sour face.

If you liked this book & got some value from it.
Would you then be so kind,
please,
to recommend it
to the people that you know.
So that they too can enjoy it
and live happier.
Thank you very much.

It was my pleasure to write and translate
this book (my third one) for you.
I hope it helps you to live happier.
(I know it will, if you do the things it teaches)

And I hope, that we can together make a contribution
to more happiness in the world.
We can.
If you recommend this book and share it.
Then I will promote it.
And together we will make a contribution to
a happier world.

I would appreciate it if you would write a short review.
Thank you for your effort.
Kind regards,
Jasmin Hajro

Met vriendelijke groeten,

Jasmin Hajro

Hajro
Ottawastraat 19
7007 BC
Doetinchem,
the Netherlands
KvK : 65686306

www.hajrobv.nl

Preview book Build your fortune

the Pay yourself first principle

It means that when you receive your money,
you first pay yourself, by for example, setting aside a tenth.
To clarify your result, we will make an example calculation.

For example, you earn 3000 euros or dollars per month.
And you pay yourself first, in other words:
you put aside a tenth (10%) of your income.
So you save 300, - euros per month.

A year has 12 months,
So after 1 year you'll have (12 x 300) = 3600, - euros.
After 1 year you have put a whole month's salary aside.

If you put aside a tenth every month,
how much will you have after 10 years?
(3600 x 10) = 36000, - euro.

So after 10 years you have 36000 euros or a whole year's salary
in your saving account.

Later on in this book: Build your Fortune, you'll see how to make
that amount that you put aside each month.
Grow faster.

Preview book Build your Fortune

10% of everything

It is important that when you first pay yourself,
by setting aside 10%.
That you put 10% of everything aside.

Of course 10% of your income.

But also 10% of the tips if you receive any,
also 10% of your surtax,
also 10% of the money you receive as a gift,
also 10% of your 13th month,
also 10% of your bonus,
also 10% of your wage increase,
also 10% of your tax refund,
also 10% of your welcome bonus,
also 10% of your holidaypay.

No matter from which angle or from whom you receive money,
the first thing you do with it,
is to pay yourself first.
By setting aside a tenth of it.

End of preview.

Preview book Moneymaker

Moneymaker 3

The bible for entrepreneurs, written by an entrepreneur. So your daily reading.
No, it's not about GOD.
It says, written by an entrepreneur .....
YOU READ ONLY BOOKS WHICH ARE WRITTEN BY PEOPLE WHO HAVE THEIR OWN COMPANY !!
Do you understand ?

This way you prevent feeding your mind with BULLSHIT.
And that you will model BULLSHIT.
So you save yourself time and money.

Ok, then a bit about that Entrepreneurial Bible.
It is called No Excuses, the Power of self discipline
And is written by Brian Tracy
And yes, he has his own company.
Otherwise his name would not be here.

It comes down to self discipline.
And self discipline makes you feel very good about yourself.
When you exercise, for example, while most people watch TV.
When you work on a Saturday, while most people have a weekend. When you take a step towards achieving your goals on Sunday.

The above 3 examples require discipline from you.
But 1, 3, 5 years from now
where will you wind up ?
And where will most people wind up ?

Have you ever worked a day with pain because your teeth were broken?
Have you ever worked with only 2 hours of sleep, the night before?
Have you ever worked without having slept the night before?

It was probably easier to watch TV then .....
But if I did, then I would be a Bullshitter for you, and not someone who you respect.
I disciplined myself and went to work.

Oh yeah, buy the entrepreneurial bible.
NOW.

Previeuw book Moneymaker

Moneymaker 2.

Two things that you have to spend your time on daily
Which 2 are they?
Watch TV and be on Facebook?

Without B.S., so:
SALES & DIRECT MARKETING
If you sell something (sales), then profit comes in.
If you become good at (direct marketing), then profit comes in.
With marketing you save yourself time while selling. You do not
have to explain who you are and what your company does during
your presentation.

How many hours per working day do you spend on sales?
How many hours per working day do You spend on Direct
Marketing?

WHAT HAPPENS IF YOU ONLY SPEND YOUR
WORKINGTIME ON SALES & DIRECT MARKETING ??

Will you have more profits and therefore more money?

End of preview
For more information about this book by me, go to
www.hajrobv.nl

<u>Small introduction with establishment Hajro</u>

Establishment Hajro is committed to helping the people in the
province of Gelderland,
by providing jobs and keeping people working,
by donating to more than 40 Charities,
and by helping people to live richer.

Today Hajro is a subsidiary of Hajro Group.
The Hajro Group consists of 19 different companies, who are all
part of 1 umbrella organization.
Called Energy Now (Energie Nu)

We now have several products & services, and we support more
than 40 charities.

Visit us at **www.hajrobv.nl**
and discover what more we can do for you.

Hopefully you will become a raving fan & customer of us.
However you choose,
I wish you
a lot of prosperity & happiness.
Kind regards,
Jasmin Hajro

Met vriendelijke groeten,

Jasmin Hajro

Hajro
Ottawastraat 19
7007 BC
Doetinchem,
the Netherlands
KvK : 65686306

www.hajrobv.nl

HAJRO

P.S. For more timesaving & profitmaking strategies,
get a copy of my book Moneymaker.